ARCTIC QUEST

HERE'S HOW TO MAKE THE MOST OF YOUR
SUPER-COOL LEGO® BOOK . . .

1.
BUILD YOUR BRAND
NEW LEGO MINIFIGURE.
IT'S ARCTIC EXPLORER
SAM SNOW, TO ADD
TO YOUR COLLECTION!

2.
READ THE STORY
OF SAM'S VERY OWN
ARCTIC ADVENTURE.

3.
SOLVE THE PUZZLES
TO FIND OUT MORE ABOUT
LIFE ON THE LEGO CITY
ARCTIC EXPEDITION!

D1630850

SEARCH AND FIND

Welcome to the Arctic! Some of the finest explorers and scientists (and dogs!) from LEGO CITY have just arrived here. Can you find them all in the scene below?

ARCTIC-5

ARCTIC-3

SAM SNOW

This explorer loves discovering new things!

JACK LENS

The best cameraman of LEGO CITY is here to capture the action.

PROFESSOR BEAGLE

A scientist with an adventurous streak!

THE HUSKIES

These dogs are strong, loyal and always hungry.

SAM'S SNOWY ADVENTURE

"Come on everybody! Let's go!"

   With a mighty roar, the crew of the LEGO CITY Arctic Expedition moved out from their camp. They were going to search for precious crystals, using their helicopter and ice crawler. Everyone was excited and ready for the day ahead. Everyone, that is, except Sam Snow. Sam had been so warm in his nice, cosy blankets that he had overslept. Everyone had left without him!

Sam rushed outside, hitched up his team of trusty huskies, and raced off on his dog sled to find his friends. At first he was able to follow the tracks of the ice crawler, but then it began to snow. Before long he could hardly see where he was going!

With the blizzard getting worse, Sam took shelter in an ice cave.
"Wow, it's really icy in here. I better be careful not to sliiiiiipppppp . . ."
With that, he slid all the way to the back of the cave. THUNK.
He hit a wall of ice and fell on his bum.

When Sam stood up and looked around, he couldn't believe what he saw. There, buried in the wall, were the biggest crystals he had ever seen.

"Amazing!" said Sam, before slipping on the ice and falling over again. "Wait until the others hear about this!"

Sam grabbed his ice pick from the sled, and started chipping the crystals out of the ice. It took him hours, but finally he succeeded! Unable to hide his delight, Sam carried his prize over to the sled. He couldn't wait to see how excited everyone back at camp would be. It had stopped snowing, too. Maybe this wasn't such a bad day after all!

It was only when Sam left the cave that he realised he had a big problem. He wasn't sure what direction to go in to get back to camp, and it was starting to get dark!

"Hmm," he said to himself. "There has to be a way I can find my way home. Someone once told me that if you're lost, you can find your way home by remembering that moss always grows on the north side of trees."

He looked around and his heart sank. There was lots of snow and ice, but no trees.

Then he had another idea. "The stars! If I can find the North Star, I can use that to guide me back to camp!"

Sam looked up at the sky, and his heart sank again. There were lots of clouds, but no stars.

"Now what am I going to do?" Sam asked himself. He was getting worried. "It's late, I'm lost and I'm getting really hungry."

"Woof!" said one of the huskies in agreement.

Suddenly, Sam started to smile. He had an idea. "Supper time!" he shouted, as loudly as he could. "Supper time!"

The dogs didn't wait around. They shot across the snow, pulling the sled behind them. Sam hung on as tightly as he could, as the dogs raced for home and a well-deserved supper.

Sam made it back to camp in no time. When he arrived back, everyone was happy to see him and the giant crystals he had found. One of his friends looked at him, scratching his head. "How did you manage to find your way home, if you were lost?"

"Oh, that was easy," Sam answered. "I asked the dogs!"

HOORAY! SAM MADE IT BACK TO THE ARCTIC CAMP, THANKS TO THE CLEVER DOGS. BUT IT'S NOT THE END OF THE EXPEDITION YET. FIND OUT WHAT ELSE HAPPENS BY SOLVING THE PUZZLES THAT FOLLOW.

TRACKS IN THE SNOW

Jack Lens is studying three photographs of footprints that have been spotted near the Arctic camp. Can you match them up to their owners?

A   B   C

QUICK WAY HOME

CAVE OF WONDERS

Deep below the icy surface, the explorers have found a huge cave full of precious crystals. Circle the ten places where the crystals can be found.

ICY MAZE

Would you like to be an Arctic explorer? Here's a little test for you. See if you can lead the ice crawler through the trenches in the snow and back to base camp.

SNOW SCIENCE

Back at base camp, Professor Beagle is carrying out a very important experiment. He has taken snow samples from three Arctic regions, and worked out that the one with the numbers one, two and four is where the most crystals are. Where should he send the explorers to?

2 5 1 8 6

4 1 2 1 5

A

C

B

8 1 1 6 4

CRYSTAL MIX-UP

It's also Professor Beagle's job to sort the crystals into the right boxes: little blue ones on the left and big grey ones on the right. Which crystals on the conveyor belt will need to be moved?

AVALANCHE!

Oh no! An avalanche has hit the base camp! Now the team needs an extra metal detector to help them find their equipment under the snow. Can you draw them a new one in the space below? Use the lines in the grid to help you.

YETI ATTACK?

Jack likes to play pranks on Sam and the Professor while they're out exploring. Put these pictures in the correct order and number them one to three, to see what he's been up to this time.

CAVE PAINTINGS

Professor Beagle has made an incredible discovery – ancient cave paintings! Can you help him with his research? Draw lines to connect the identical pairs of symbols.

21

ON THIN ICE

Collecting crystals can be dangerous work when there is ice around. Can you find a route that will help Sam collect these ones without falling through a hole? Draw a line that both begins and ends at the 'START' box.

START

Clues:

No entry

Enter only once

KITTING UP

Arctic explorers need lots of equipment. Jack, Sam and the Professor all have similar items, but each of them has one item that the other two don't. Can you spot what it is for each minifigure?

SLIPPERY SLOPE

Sam has an important sample to deliver to the Professor, but doesn't want to end up skidding all the way down the hill to base camp! Put a tick next to each of the items below that he might use to help him.

ALONE IN THE DARK

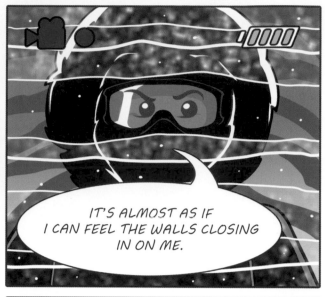

SNOW STORM

A snow storm has hit! A polar bear is coming! Professor Beagle doesn't even have a hat! He needs to find shelter, and quickly. Draw in the igloo, using the grey lines as a guide, so that he can huddle up inside.

NIGHT WATCH

Some polar bears have been spotted nearby, and it's your shift on night watch. Take a look through the night vision device and circle any polar bears you see.

MARKS IN THE SNOW

Jack has dropped his favourite video camera from the helicopter! Help him find it by looking for the correct shape in the snow.

SNOWBALL RACE

It's the end of a successful expedition, and the explorers are having fun with a snowball race. Who managed to roll the biggest snowball? Follow the lines to find the winner!

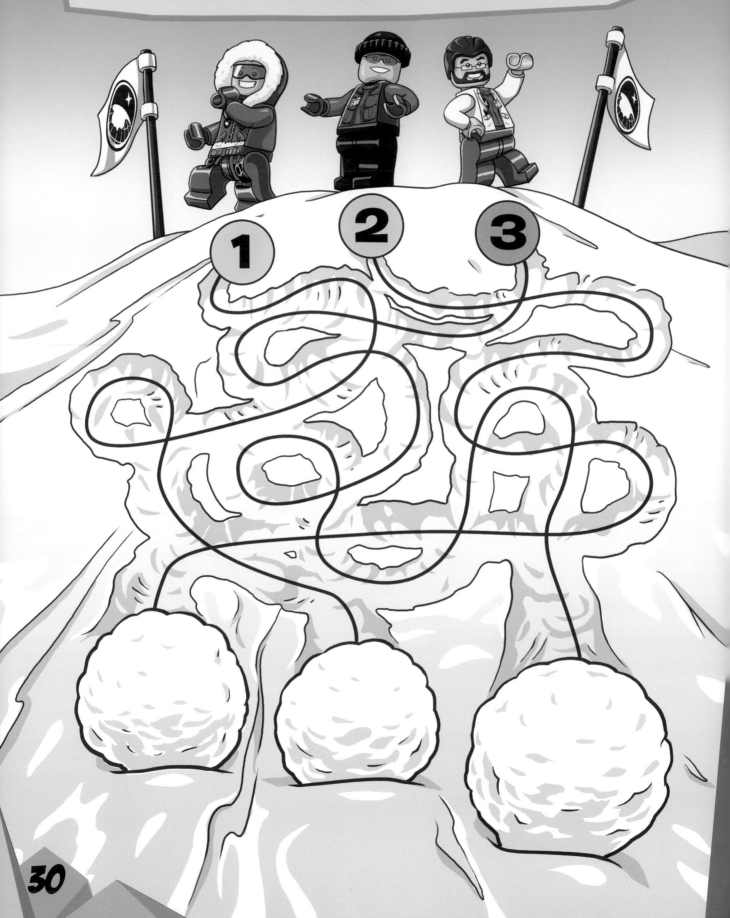

ANSWERS

p. 2-3 SEARCH AND FIND

p. 12 TRACKS IN THE SNOW

p. 14-15 CAVE OF WONDERS

p. 16 ICY MAZE

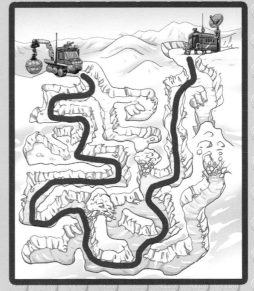

p. 17 SNOW SCIENCE

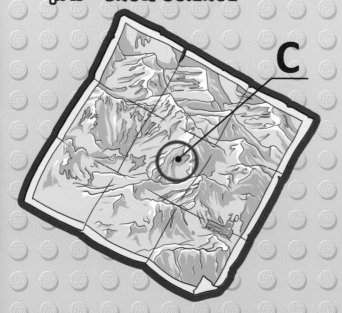

p. 18 CRYSTAL MIX-UP

p.20 YETI ATTACK?

p.21 CAVE PAINTINGS

p.22-23 ON THIN ICE

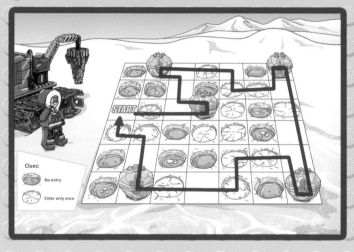

p.24 KITTING UP

p.25 SLIPPERY SLOPE

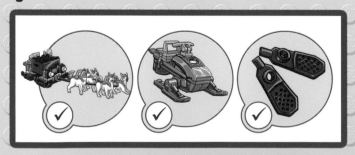

p.29 MARKS IN THE SNOW

p.28 NIGHT WATCH

p.30 3